EXPLAINING ADHD – A PAEDIATRICIAN TALKS TO PARENTS

R. M. BERGH, MDCM, FRCPC

Cover and book design by Gauvin Press.
Printed and bound in Canada at Gauvin Press.

National Library of Canada Cataloguing in Publication Data

Bergh. R. M. (Rodney M.), 1928-
Explaining ADHD : a paediatrician talks to parents / R. M. Bergh.

Includes index.
ISBN 0-9736020-0-7

1. Attention-deficit hyperactivity disorder – Popular works.
I. Title.

RJ506.H9B46 2004   618.92'8589   C2004-905099-0

Nicro Publishing
Ottawa, Ontario, Canada

DEDICATION

This book would not have been possible without the urging and encouragement of my wife, Nicole, and without the support and skills of our friend, Mary LeBlanc. Perhaps most importantly, it has been my patients and their families who have taught me about ADHD in real life. I have had the pleasure of sharing with them the satisfaction that comes from seeing a child quite quickly begin to experience success.

The author would like to deny any resemblance between him and the pictures in this book, but among other things, they all lack hair, they all…

SOME POINTS TO BE DISCUSSED

- ADHD is not diagnosed or treated because of hyperactivity.

- ADHD is hereditary.

- ADHD does not stop when one walks out the school doors and often interferes with social success.

- ADHD frequently continues into the adult years.

- Medication has to be considered when treatment is indicated, as no other approach is as effective. However, other support may be both helpful and necessary along with medication.

- Treatment of ADHD from the early school years can contribute greatly to reducing or preventing behaviour problems for the teenager and adult.

Parents bring their children to my office because they have genuine concerns about their child's future and someone – either one or both parents, a teacher or the family physician – has raised the question of ADHD. This possibility is often frightening and sometimes resisted or rejected by parents (we all like to believe that there is nothing wrong with our children). Some parents greet me with the statement that they would like to know if their child has ADHD but would never consider medication. Some parents come only because "The school has forced them to do so."

Mothers often have more involvement with their children than fathers and are more likely to be the ones who have received the telephone calls from the teacher. Mothers tend to have more contact with the children during the day and may be more aware of difficulties between siblings or with other children at school or in the neighbourhood.

On the other hand, a decision about medical treatment for a child should be made by both parents based on thorough understanding of the condition and the pros and cons of treatment options. It is therefore my strong recommendation that both parents be present for the initial evaluation of a child for ADHD so that all questions and concerns may be addressed.

If any medication is to be used for any condition, parents and child must be comfortable with the diagnosis and with the medication and the reasons for its use.

It is often the difficulties in school that first make people wonder about ADHD, but the same difficulties will also affect the child at home and in interaction with other children. The impact may not be as obvious in the social area, at least in the younger years, but this impact on everyday life eventually has a greater negative impact on self-esteem, self-confidence and overall success than any academic failure.

Over the years I have learned much from my patients and their families and have gained an understanding of people's concerns about ADHD and the medications used to treat it. The information I am going to give to you should answer most, if not all, of your questions and concerns and will help you recognize what is accurate information and what is not. It is my hope that this will allow you to be more comfortable with the decisions you may have to make about your child.

Identification and treatment of ADHD does not guarantee success because there are many other factors that can affect one's outcome. However, ADHD by itself can be a major contributor to failure to develop self-esteem, self-assurance and self-confidence. We can do something very effective to address that part of a problem.

By identifying and treating ADHD I believe that we can help to prevent many of the behaviour problems that can arise in the teen years. For example, many people in jail or otherwise in trouble with the law have ADHD that was not properly treated. I think we can change that.

The frequency of ADHD (3-7%) does not seem to have changed in many years but as people become more aware of it, more children are being recognized as having it. To give an idea of how significant this can be, let's look at a grade school that has 350 pupils. In that population, there will be 10 - 25 pupils who will not do as well as they should in learning because they have ADHD. Half of these children are also at risk for severe behaviour problems from ADHD as teenagers. The other half may also have behaviour problems but to a less severe degree. From the point of view of those in public health, these figures quickly become impressive, and even alarming, when they are applied to the population figures of large communities.

This presentation is an attempt to give you accurate information about ADHD in a form that explains the scientific information in a way that can be applied to a family.

ADHD is a diagnosis any parent dreads to hear. We always knew our son was very unique, and a real challenge. For us, learning our son is diagnosed with Attention Deficit Hyperactivity Disorder, this helps us better understand why our child behaves, interacts and learns the way he does. With lots of love, continued unconditional acceptance and the proper treatment in place (365 days of the year), we can see our child developing into a more social, focussed, and much happier little guy who is now learning to better manage his own behaviour – this is a real gift for the whole family

Parents of a grade school boy

CHAPTER I
ADHD – WHAT IT IS

Attention Deficit Hyperactivity Disorder (ADHD) has a bad reputation for various reasons. One of these reasons is that many people continue to think that the diagnosis is based on the 'hyperactivity' part of the name – that children are diagnosed because of overactivity and treated to calm them down. This is completely wrong – I do not diagnose children on the basis of activity levels and the medicines we use do not calm or quiet. Hyperactivity in some cases can be so extreme that a child can be literally "climbing the walls", but it may also be simply fidgeting, playing with a pencil, not able to sit still, etc. – if this activity is more marked than in the average person, it is still called 'hyperactivity'. Overactivity is often what is noticed first because it can be so annoying to others. It tends to decrease in severity as one gets older and, in the teenager or adult, may be simply a feeling of restlessness.

It was previously thought that ADHD was different from ADD (inattentiveness without the hyperactivity) and many parents are rather upset by the term ADHD because they do not see their child as being overactive. I don't think it matters a great deal whether or not the "H" is there, as it is not an important part of the disorder or the reason for treatment. Because most people with the disorder do have some degree of hyperactivity, I will use the term

ADHD, recognizing that the "H" can vary from none at all to very severe.

Girls with ADHD generally have much less hyperactivity than boys do and will often seem to be listening because they are sitting quietly; however while they are sitting and looking at the teacher, their minds are often somewhere else. Teachers may therefore not be able to recognize them as easily as overactive boys, and this may be one factor that contributes to the idea that ADHD is four or five times more common in boys than in girls. It would appear that many girls with ADHD have been missed because they were not overactive, yet had features of inattentiveness and/or impulsivity.

To determine whether or not ADHD may be present, we look for characteristics that come from being unable – and I use the word 'unable' on purpose – unable to organize thinking. The person with ADHD has a hard time paying attention, concentrating, or focusing, is easily distracted and tends to be very impulsive. Hyperactivity is very often a part of the picture but, in my view, is not the basis of the diagnosis or the treatment.

It has been proposed that ADHD be divided into three categories – those with primarily inattention, those with primarily hyperactivity and impulsivity and those with a combination of all three. This categorization may be more applicable to adults as, in my practice, I have found that most children have a combination of all the characteristics. In any event, when medication is indicated, the same ones are used, regardless of the category.

Children who have ADHD are born with it; it is not something that develops. If the features only show up after a few years in school and seem to be something new, it may be some other condition imitating ADHD rather than ADHD itself. There is more and more evidence being uncovered to show that ADHD is a genetic disorder – it is hereditary, or passed on from generation to generation. One can frequently follow it down through the generations in a family.

The diagnosis of ADHD is made by determining whether certain criteria, or requirements are met. As the name says, we are trying to determine whether or not the child has a shorter than normal attention span. Because all children have a short attention span in the pre-school years, it is almost impossible to diagnose ADHD with any degree of certainty until the child has started school. Once a child gets into school the ability to sit to focus and concentrate should begin to develop. Teachers have an advantage in identifying this disorder because they have a fairly large group of children who are at the same age and same stage of learning and who are mostly average children. They therefore have a very good idea of what is normal for each level in school. The children who fall outside the 'norm' will be more easily identified by the teacher because of the bigger basis for comparison. Often the child is first identified because of the difficulty in controlling him/her in class because of the hyperactivity. As has been said, this is only a warning sign and not the basis for the diagnosis.

ADHD has nothing to do with race, nationality, intelligence or social or economic status. Some people have the idea that children with ADHD are slow learners. This is absolutely incorrect and intelligence in these children can vary, like other children, from below average to superior. I have seen children from many races and parts of the world with ADHD. The acceptance of the diagnosis and its treatment can certainly vary from culture to culture. Cultural beliefs are very strong and deep-rooted and can make it difficult for some parents to recognize and feel comfortable with the idea of giving a medication for so many years for such a condition. I cannot emphasize strongly enough the benefit to the child that comes from an improved ability to use one's brain better in all situations. Until recently, the disorder has been diagnosed more in North America, but there seems to be increasing recognition of its presence in other parts of the world.

CHAPTER II
CONSIDERATIONS FOR TREATING

The disorder was first identified over fifty years ago. For the first forty of those fifty years it was felt that the only reason to treat children with ADHD was to help them learn, and for many, many years, children with ADHD were treated only on school days. Those children did better academically but their long-term outcomes as teenagers were no better than if they had had no treatment at all.

It was realized that half the children with ADHD who are not treated at all will end up in their teen years with very severe behavior disorders – lying, stealing, cheating, running away from home, dropping out of school, and unfortunately, frequently being in trouble with the law. Children treated on school days only did better in school but had exactly the same risks for teenage behaviour problems as if they had not been treated at all.

There are other causes for behaviour problems – ADHD is only one of them but it is one that can be well and quickly helped, especially if it is identified early. Think of the loss to society in terms of dysfunctional individuals and stressed families, the financial costs of trying to help and support these individuals and the costs of crime itself. THERE IS EVERY REASON TO BELIEVE THAT WE COULD PREVENT A SIGNIFICANT PORTION OF TEENAGE AND ADULT BEHA-

VIOUR DISORDERS IF WE COULD IDENTIFY AND TREAT ALL CHILDREN WITH ADHD-RELATED DIFFICULTIES IN THEIR EARLY YEARS IN SCHOOL.

It was recognized and realized that this poor long-term result was happening but was not really understood until the late 1980's and early 1990's. The behaviours leading to these poor outcomes are not an integral part of ADHD but they develop because of the low self-esteem and self-worth that results from what ADHD does to you.

We all need to be liked and accepted by others, we need to be socially successful. People who are not socially successful tend to have low self-esteem – if other people don't like you, it is very difficult to like yourself. I believe that it is this low self-esteem that contributes most strongly to the behavioral problems that develop in the teen years in so many children with inadequately or untreated ADHD.

ADHD is one of the conditions that can interfere with one's ability to get along well with others. The children treated only on school days did better academically but nothing was being done to help them in their everyday contacts and activities. They therefore had the same social problems as those children who were not treated at all, the same low self esteem and the same poor long-term outcome. While academic success is important, it does not contribute as much to self-esteem as social success.

It is now felt that there are two reasons for treating ADHD: – THE ACADEMIC ONE that had been recognized for forty years, and, I think even more importantly, THE SOCIAL ONE, because the child is able to think better in every-day contacts. Therefore it has been recommended since 1994 that treatment be given seven days a week, year round to improve the chances of success both academically and socially. Within weeks of starting treatment for

ADHD one can see the improvement in self-esteem as the child begins to be able to interact better with peers and family, simply because he can think better. Success in school is certainly important, but low self-esteem and the resulting poor attitudes and behaviour problems can put even someone with a top university degree at risk of ending up only as a smart crook.

CHAPTER III

ADHD – ITS EFFECT

As we all know, children can be very cruel to others. If there is something about a child that the others do not like, there is very little hesitation in pushing that child aside and rejecting him. ADHD is one of the conditions that can result in this rejection.

The child with ADHD who has been pushed aside has two options – remain with other children who have also been pushed aside; or, as a way of becoming accepted by peers, to become the 'class clown". This will improve acceptance by classmates but will only be effective for a few years, as 'class clowns' are not as well accepted in the high school years. In the early school years, it is one method that can help achieve social success. When the child with ADHD who is the 'class clown' is started on therapy and becomes accepted in his own right, he usually stops being the 'class clown' quite quickly. Being 'class clown' may result from a type of personality but it is more often an indication that a child is having difficulties with peer relationships, and should not be ignored.

Children with ADHD have a hard time recognizing the consequences of their actions. The impulsivity and the difficulty in organizing their thoughts often leads to an inability to realize what effect the things they say or do may have on other people. They know the consequences if you sit down and talk to them but

THEY ACT BEFORE THEY THINK. THE VERY FIRST DAY THEY GO ON TREATMENT, THEY WILL BE ABLE TO THINK BEFORE THEY ACT. They will immediately be less likely to say or do things that may not be appropriate. This will immediately improve their ability to interact with others.

Every child, when first starting school, goes with excitement and enthusiasm – everyone wants to learn and tries to learn. If anything interferes with success when you try, you will eventually stop trying. If one reaches for the proverbial bar and never grabs it, he will stop trying. If one tries in school and doesn't succeed, he will eventually stop trying there. If the cause of the problem is not recognized, the child is often labeled as 'not interested', 'not motivated', 'doesn't care', 'doesn't try', and sometimes 'lazy', 'dumb', or 'stupid'. If the child is actually trying very hard and is not 'lazy', 'dumb', or 'stupid', the impact on self-esteem is even worse.

Because of these factors, I think we have a much better chance for success as teenagers if we can identify and treat children with ADHD before they are eight to ten years old. The longer a child goes on with lack of success and low self-esteem, the more deep-seated the resulting behaviors and attitudes will become and the more difficult they will be to change in later years.

The child with ADHD and above average intelligence may be missed if only class marks are used as a measure of scholastic success. Up to grade six, these children don't have to concentrate long to learn. They can therefore produce good marks in the early years without having to focus. When they get to grade seven, eight or nine and the work becomes more difficult, they will tend to have more problems academically. However, in evaluating ADHD, we are not looking at marks – the 'outcome' of learning - but how you learn – the 'process' of learning

Young children usually want and try to please their parents and are delighted when they are praised and thanked for something they have done. This is what builds self-esteem. A child with ADHD very often needs reminding and sometimes pressure to be able to start a task that she has been asked to do. She often will get side-tracked in the process and need reminding to be able to complete that task. A child may sometimes need a parent to work directly with her to do a job. Praise and thanks for this sort of supervised effort does not give the same pleasure as praise and thanks for a job done by the child on her own.

Self esteem is something we earn—it cannot be taught or given.

CHAPTER IV
ADHD – THE BASIC PROBLEM

We don't really know what ADHD is, as we cannot take out a piece of the brain, examine and test it, and then glue it back in. Current thinking is that it is one of a group of conditions called Neurotransmitter Disorders, a group of disorders where patches of cells in the brain cannot work normally because of a biochemical dysfunction in those cells. The chemicals involved are those used in sending signals back and forth from cell to cell – the neurotransmitters- dopamine, serotonin and nor-epinephrine.

Other disorders which are thought to be caused by a neurotransmitter disorder are Parkinson's Disease, Autism, Bipolar Disorder, Schizophrenia, etc. Much research and study is being carried out to try to better understand these conditions as well. There may be some overlap in symptoms between these various conditions, but there are significant and specific differences between them.

In the research on ADHD, a number of different instruments have been used to try to measure and understand brain function. One of the early ones was a PET Scanner, a machine which measures certain waves given off by the brain. In those studies, it was found that when a PET Scan was done of the brain of an individual with ADHD, very specific areas in the brain were identified where the cells could not use the sugar that was present for their energy. All our cells burn sugar for energy – it is the fuel for our body. These cells could not get the energy they needed to function properly. When these people were treated, the PET Scan became normal in appearance. Even with the first dose of medicine, one can often see the effects of being able to think better in about thirty minutes

More recent studies continue to add further evidence to show that there are measurable differences, both in structure and in function, in some areas of the brain in the person with untreated ADHD when compared with the brain in people without ADHD or with ADHD that has been treated.

To explain ADHD to children, the analogy that I use is that of a computer that is plugged in but in which there is a small problem with the wiring. When I ask a child how well that computer will work, the usual response is 'not well' or 'not properly'. I give that response a more positive approach and point out that 'it will work, but not as well as it should'. When you have ADHD, the computer in your head (the brain) is plugged in but there is a problem with the wiring in very small areas inside. It will work, but not as well as it should. When children have this problem, it is not their fault – this is the way the computer was put together before they were born. When they have this problem, no matter how hard they try, (and most children start out trying very hard), they cannot make the computer work properly. However, there is a medication that acts as a computer technician and fixes the wiring in the computer. Children seem to understand and accept this explanation very well and it demonstrates very well to parents that the only thing we do when we treat ADHD is to LET the child think better. What they do with it when they can think better is up to the child and to the parents.

For many children, especially those identified in the earlier school years, the improved ability to think allows them to become more successful. When behaviour problems continue or there are other factors contributing to the overall difficulty, it is very important for the child and family to receive counselling. Many teenagers are reluctant to do this, but the child is the only one who can change his own behaviours and attitudes. Other people can be of help, but the child has to want to change.

It used to be thought that everyone with ADHD would 'outgrow' it in their late teens or early twenties. It is now realized that this is not accurate. Sixty to seventy percent of people with ADHD will continue to have the characteristics into the adult years. They do tend to get a little less severe and some will disappear – the hyperactivity for example, tends to become much less severe. However for two thirds of patients, the characteristics will continue into adulthood to some degree and ADHD is recently being identified and treated in increasing numbers of adults. It is being recognized that about 3% of adults have ADHD as a significant factor contributing to their problems.

This is not to suggest that all adults with ADHD warrant treatment, but if they continue to have problems, medical treatment should be considered as one of their options. The characteristics tend to become less severe, and, as adults, many people can develop other ways of organizing themselves. For example, many adults with ADHD become great list-makers or use diaries, agendas, etc to help organize their time and activities. However, adults can better recognize the effect of medication and a significant number choose to go on, or to stay on, treatment as adults.

CHAPTER V

ADHD – ITS PRESENTATION AND DIAGNOSIS

Unfortunately there is no specific test that can be done to diagnose ADHD – no blood test, no x-ray, etc. The diagnosis cannot be made on the basis of a physical examination, interview, or observation of the patient. There is no specific psychological test that can be done to make the diagnosis. The diagnosis is made when established criteria or requirements are met. These look primarily at two questions: are there enough of the characteristics present for a period of more than six months, and have they been present since before age seven. These criteria have been developed and published by the American Psychiatric Association in the Diagnostic and Statistical Manual Of Mental Disorders (DSM) and are reviewed and updated periodically, with the most recent published in 1994. The diagnosis is therefore based on information gathered from the patient's history, questionnaires and report cards. (See TABLE 1) Psychologists can gather this same information and can come to the same conclusion but, as mentioned above, there is no specific test that can confirm the diagnosis. It would certainly make the job of evaluating these children much easier if a specific test were available.

ATTENTION DEFICIT / HYPERACTIVITY DISORDER

DSM – IV Symptom Questionnaire				
ITEMS	Not at all	Just a Little	Pretty Much	Very Much
1. Fails to give close attention to details or makes careless mistakes in schoolwork, work, or other activities.				
2. Difficulty in sustaining attention in tasks or play activities.				
3. Does not seem to listen when spoken to directly.				
4. Does not follow through on instructions and fails to finish schoolwork, chores or duties in the workplace (not due to oppositional behaviour or failure to understand instructions)/				
5. Difficulty organizing talks and activities.				
6. Avoids, dislikes, or is reluctant to engage in tasks that require sustained mental effort (such as schoolwork or homework).				
7. Loses things necessary for tasks or activities (e.g. toys, school assignments, pencils, books, or tools).				
8. Easily distracted by extraneous stimuli.				
9. Forgetful in daily activities.				
10. Fidgets with hands or feet or squirms in seat.				
11. Leaves seat in classroom or in other situations in which remaining seated is expected.				
12. Runs about or climbs excessively in situations in which it is inappropriate (in adolescents or adults, may be limited to subjective feelings of restlessness).				
13. Difficulty playing or engaging in leisure activities quietly.				
14. Is 'on the go" or often acts as if 'driven by a motor'.				
15. Talks excessively.				
16. Blurts out answers before questions have been completed.				
17. Has difficulty awaiting turn.				
18. Interrupts or intrudes on others (e.g., butts into conversations or games)				

Table 1: DSM - IV Symptom Questionnaire

These are the characteristics that are looked at and rated to evaluate ADHD. Having such information from parents and teachers is a necessary part of the total information required but, by itself, is not enough to make the diagnosis. Were these characteristics present before seven years of age and are they present in school and out?

Report cards provide very important evidence for the evaluation because there is usually a different teacher each year who can compare and comment on the child in comparison to a group of mostly average children. When we see comments in the report cards year after year that characteristics of ADHD interfere with the child's ability to learn and function in school, this is very strong support for the diagnosis. This is not a scientific process and is not 100% accurate (most scientific tests are actually not 100% accurate either) but when the total evidence allows a comfortable 'Yes' response to the questions (enough characteristics present since before age seven in school and out), one can be at least 90-95% accurate.

It must be remembered that ADHD is not the only condition that can cause these symptoms. During the evaluation of the child who has difficulties in these areas, one must consider whether or not there is evidence to suggest that other causes must also be considered. As with ADHD, most of these other conditions cannot be diagnosed with a specific test and it is sometimes difficult to be scientifically precise. It is for this reason that I say that one cannot be 100% accurate in the diagnosis.

Until the mid-1990s it was felt that ADHD was primarily a school problem. It is now realized that the characteristics do not stop as you walk out the school doors and the condition must be shown to be causing difficulties in the non-school setting as well (at home, with peers, etc). This sometimes leads to some difficulty in being comfortable with the diagnosis, as the home situation is less demanding for focus and concentration. There are fewer distractions within the home. Parents have often recognized and learned to manage problems that a child may have had in interacting within the family. When evaluating a child to determine whether or not there is a significant problem, one has to ask, 'How well can the child do on his own?' rather than 'How well can he do with my help?'

Teachers are often the first people to recognize that a child is having problems that may be due to ADHD and will often be the first to raise the possibility to the parents. The hyperactivity and difficulty in controlling the child in class may be what is first noted by the teacher. The child may be unable to sit still to work as well as classmates, may be very easily distracted by other things going on in the room, and may disrupt classmates by fidgeting, making noises etc. These children often need to have instructions repeated to them on an individual basis before being able to understand what is being asked of them. They frequently forget to take their homework with them, and homework often includes unfinished classroom work as well as the usual assigned work. The child frequently needs one-on-one support from a parent to be able to get the work done at home, even though distractions are kept to a minimum. Many children will begin to hide their homework or lie about having any, and getting them to sit to do it becomes an all-out battle.

In the home setting, children with ADHD may be less interested or less able to sit to colour and draw, and may have difficulty in completing a picture, sometimes flitting from one activity to another. They may be more interested in, and therefore more able, to play Lego, work on the computer and play computer games. They will often have difficulty in being able to respond the first time to a request to do something at home - picking up toys, cleaning up the bedroom, taking dishes to the kitchen - and often need reminding to be able to stay on task because they are so easily side-tracked by television, toys, other children or even their own thoughts. These children sometimes have more difficulty getting along well with siblings or with children in the neighbourhood. They often require more supervision or create more worry about their play outdoors because of their inability to recognize danger in a play situation or because they may impulsively dart out onto the road in front of an oncoming car.

Children with ADHD are often noted to rush through school work, homework or tasks at school or at home and they end up with work that is poorly done or sloppy. In their report cards there may be comments about not editing or rereading their work.

They will often be identified as having difficulty in their written work and in composing stories. In fact, the ideas are in their heads but the child often cannot organize them well enough to write them down. They may also have difficulty organizing thoughts to be able to express them verbally.

It is in school also that it may be first recognized that the child is having problems in relationships with classmates – plays roughly – aggressive – not able to share well or to take turns. This behaviour is more likely to be unintentional than willful, at least initially. It is sometimes said that these children 'don't know when to stop' and can be annoying to others because of this.

In the kindergarten years, teachers try to avoid making negative comments about their students because they are in a transition phase and are only just beginning to develop the ability to focus and pay attention. Some teachers in later years in school are also very reluctant about making any comments because some of them have received very negative reaction from the parents when the possibility has been raised. Some parents feel that teachers simply want their students to sit quietly in front of them and that this is the only reason that treatment is being suggested. To be fair to teachers, I think most are there because they want to teach. When they have a student who seems quite capable, but cannot learn because of a treatable condition, I think most teachers prefer to see that child identified, treated properly and allowed to develop normally. The behaviours and needs of the inattentive child will also interfere with the teacher's ability to teach the other children.

The pressures on students and teachers are greater now than they were a generation ago - class sizes are bigger, there is a constant increase in the amount of material to learn and one can no longer get a good job without a high school education. Many children with untreated ADHD simply used to drop out of school and yet were still able to find work. However, many have had a very hard time holding a job and have tended to move from one job to another.

When a child has a problem in learning, there are three broad groups of conditions that can contribute to this.

I.   ADHD
II. LEARNING DISABILITIES
III. SLOW LEARNERS

I. Because children with ADHD are not able to pay attention and concentrate on their work, they will not be able to learn as well. The disorder is not rare. At least three to seven percent of children have ADHD. More recently it has been suggested that the frequency may be even higher as it is being better recognized. In any event, there has not been an increase in the frequency in the fifty years since it was first recognized. This amounts to one to three children with ADHD in every class.

II. The second group consists of those children who have what are called 'Learning Disabilities' – conditions where intelligence is normal, but one specific part of the brain that is used in learning does not function properly. Dyslexia is the example of a learning disability that most people have heard of. If you have dyslexia you have normal intelligence and normal eyesight, but the part of the brain that interprets squiggles and turns them into letters, words, numbers, and gives them meaning does not work well. Learning disabilities are even more common than ADHD. Ten to twenty percent of children will have a learning disability.

III. The third group consists of those children who are slow learners and who just need more time to learn. There are several conditions that can result in a general delay in the ability to learn.

The three conditions are all so common in their own right that twenty-five percent of children with ADHD will have another problem interfering with learning. Therefore identification of ADHD does not necessarily mean that we have identified all the reasons that a child may have difficulty in learning. However, treatment of the ADHD will allow the child to focus better. When difficulties persist, the child may need further evaluation to determine and address co-existing factors.

I realize now that our youngest child has always shown the classic signs of ADHD, but hindsight is always 20/20. His behaviour was not as extreme as a lot of other children that I had seen but our son was definitely more active and impulsive than his four much older siblings. I knew right from the beginning that he was going to be a challenge. A few bold friends and relatives even expressed the opinion that he was spoiled because I was a much older mother now and didn't have the energy or patience. Because he was a very bright and respectful little boy who could sit for hours at activities which he really enjoyed, it never even occurred to his father and me to suspect ADHD. My first clue came when he was running down the hall in school and I jokingly said to his third grade teacher, "maybe he has ADHD." I was stunned when she replied; "You might want to have that checked out." Apparently teachers are not allowed to suggest such a thing to parents but may comment if the parent brings up the topic first.

My husband was not very open to the idea but, because it was so important to me, he agreed to take our son to a psychologist for an assessment. We received a document which indicated that ADHD was the problem. The psychologist suggested to us that we might want to consider medication as well as behaviour modification. The medication aspect was not well explained and, as with most parents, we did not want our child to be 'drugged'. For the next three years, our son struggled through school with lots of help from us with the enormous amount of homework he had because he wasn't getting the work done during school hours. We also put out thousands of dollars for tutors and a learning center which promised to help him learn to do the work on his own. Nothing worked and I was at the end of my rope. I could tell that he wasn't being lazy or defiant – he simply could not stay focussed. I felt like I was doing my grade 6 all over again and that if medication was not going to be an option for our son, it might have to be an option for me!

When I went to our family doctor about the problem, we were referred to a paediatrician. We were immediately put at ease with a common sense explanation of ADHD and were given statistics on how many people are affected. We were told that the medication (Dexedrine) had been used for many years and is safe. We were told that a diagnosis could be made with a 95% accuracy rate based on the teachers' comments over the years on our son's report cards as well as the questionnaires that parents and current teachers are asked to complete. We were told that we could try one dose of the medication and that we would know within half an hour if he was correctly diagnosed because he would be "high" if he was not. We really wondered at first if he was misdiagnosed because he was so giddy and delighted at the effects of those tablets. He must have thanked us fifty times that morning for helping him and told us that for the first time in his life he was able to think about only one thing at a time and immediately felt more coordinated.

Our son's teacher told me that he had previous experience with ADHD kids who were on the medication and some who were not, but he had never had a child in his class who went on the medication mid-way through the school year. He could not believe the immediate change for the better. The medication has also helped our son in sports. He had been a mediocre hockey player at best but has vastly improved. He took the very first dose on the morning of a practice and was asked by one of the better players if he had taken speed skating lessons. The other hockey parents could not believe the improvement in his game. Perhaps the most important benefit though has been in his personal relationships. The medication has not altered his basic personality in any way but our son is no longer so impulsive and his behaviour is always more appropriate now. This is an obvious advantage when it comes to friendships and getting along better with others.

As with anything, there are drawbacks though. The medication made our son feel nauseous for the first week but the benefits were so great to him that he insisted on taking the full dose until his body adjusted. He also experienced a decreased appetite and though he needed to lose a considerable amount of weight, it is important to make sure he gets the nutrition that he needs to grow. His desire for junk food has dramatically decreased. All in all, the plusses far outweigh the negatives.

Mother of a teenager

CHAPTER VI
ADHD AND BEHAVIOUR PROBLEMS

Many children with untreated ADHD will develop significant behaviour problems, primarily, I believe, because the condition interferes with social success, which results in low self-esteem. Academic success is not as important as social success, even into adolescence. Other problems can interfere with social success and cause low self-esteem but there is no other condition that can be treated so efficiently and so effectively with medication.

Most children have the desire and ability to make friends easily and often very quickly. I have seen two or three children meet for the first time in my waiting room and be happily playing with each other in minutes. When a child doesn't have that ability, for whatever reason, that child begins to feel unsure of himself and before long, when the child has no friends or fights all the time with siblings and other children, self esteem becomes very low. The child will begin to develop behaviours and attitudes in response to this unhappy situation. Such behaviours only tend to make the child even more unacceptable to others.

The first group of behaviours that tend to develop when a child has difficult relationships is called Oppositional and Defiance Disorder (ODD). (see Table 3) These children lose their tempers easily, protect their egos by blaming other people for their problems or lie and will begin to argue and become defiant. ADHD is one of the conditions that can interfere with the development of good relationships with other people. I think that this is the more important reason to treat ADHD, for if nothing is done to correct the problem at this level, the behaviours tend to get worse as the child becomes older and develop into the more severe problems of Conduct Disorder, problems which put teenagers at great risk of very poor outcomes.

The behaviours that are included in Conduct Disorders are much more severe and involve physical aggression, stealing, damaging property and law breaking. Many of the people in jail or otherwise in trouble with the law have ADHD that was not properly treated.

Statistics can be very boring but also very enlightening and I am going to try to give you some in a way that will show how much impact ADHD can have if not recognized and addressed.

In a study of children with ADHD who were compared to a group of similar children without ADHD, sexual intercourse started at 15 as compared to 16 and these children had more sexual partners (19 as compared to7). There were more pregnancies in the ADHD group (38% as compared to 4%) and more sexually transmitted diseases (17% as against 4%). The frequency of HIV infection was significantly greater in the ADHD group as compared to those without (54% to 21%)

A few more figures. As I have stated, if ADHD is not treated, there is a grave risk that behaviours of Oppositional and Defiance Disorder and Conduct Disorder will follow. The resulting risk for legal problems is illustrated by these facts: Persons with ADHD are more likely to be arrested (39% vs. 20%), more likely to be arrested more than once (23% vs. 8%), convicted of a crime (28% vs. 11%) and more likely to be jailed (9% vs 1%).

CHECKLIST TO EVALUATE OPPOSITIONAL AND DEFIANCE DISORDER				
ITEMS	Not at all	Just a Little	Pretty Much	Very Much
19. Loses temper.				
20. Argues with adults.				
21. Actively defies or refuses to comply with adult's requests or rules.				
22. Deliberately annoys people.				
23. Blames others for his or her mistakes or misbehaviour.				
24. Touchy or easily annoyed by others.				
25. Angry and resentful.				
26. Spiteful or vindictive.				
CHECKLIST TO EVALUATE CONDUCT DISORDER				
27. Initiates physical fights				
28. Has used a weapon that can cause serious physical harm to others (e.g., a bat, brick, broken bottle, knife, gun).				
29. Has been physically cruel to people.				
30. Has been physically cruel to animals.				
31. Has stolen while confronting a victim (e.g., mugging, purse snatching, extortion, armed robbery).				
32. Has deliberately engaged in fire setting with the intention of causing serious damage.				
33. Has deliberately destroyed others' property (other than by fire setting).				
34. Has broken into someone else's house, building, or car.				
35. Lies to obtain goods or favours or to avoid obligations (i.e., 'cons' others).				
36. Has stolen items of nontrivial value without confronting a victim (e.g., shoplifting, but without breaking and entering; forgery)				
37. Stays out at night despite parental prohibitions, beginning before age 13 years.				
38. Has run away from home overnight at least twice while living in parental or parental surrogate home (or once without returning for a lengthy period).				
39. Truant from school, beginning before age 13 years.				

Table 2: Evaluation Checklists

When we start children on treatment at an early enough age and other things being equal (i.e. - nothing else contributing to the lack of success), the behaviour problems of Oppositional and Defiance Disorder can shift from severe to minimal in a two-month period. When we diagnose and treat ADHD, it is not because of these behaviours. When one improves the underlying problem and allows the child to become more successful in society, the reason for the behaviours disappears as self-esteem rises. ODD is not part of ADHD but the result of the difficulty in being successful in social and academic endeavours because of the characteristics of ADHD. In my view, this is much the more important reason to treat ADHD and is the reason that treatment is indicated seven days a week, every day of the year, in school and out. To repeat – by treating, we don't make the child do better, we don't help the child do better – we let the child do better.

Let me emphasize that the treatment of ADHD with medication does not directly alter or correct behaviour. It is also worth repeating that many other factors can contribute to behaviour problems and that the longer the inappropriate behaviours have been present, the more difficult they will be to change. Medication along with good parenting may well be all that is required for some children with ADHD but for others, behaviour management and professional counselling will be important parts of therapy.

CHAPTER VII
ADHD – WHAT TREATMENT CAN DO

When a child with ADHD starts treatment we usually see some amazing results. I have seen children up to grade VI, who, at the end of the second term in February or March, were destined to fail. With treatment, they passed in June. Many children can leave their special education programs and return to their regular classes. For the older child, you can almost guarantee that marks will go up 15-20%. These children are no smarter - their 'computers' are now working the way they are supposed to. Treatment of the ADHD will, of course, have no direct effect on any other learning problem that may accompany the ADHD.

Some children with ADHD have poor fine motor skills. Children in grade one are generally able to colour pictures within the lines and are beginning to print well. Many children can colour within the lines even in the pre-school years. Letter reversals when printing should disappear while in grade one or two.

For some reason that I don't yet understand, many children with ADHD will have a remarkable improvement in fine-motor skills on the first day they go on treatment. From one day to the next, printing or writing can change from being unreadable to beautiful and a child can change from a scribbler to being able to colour beautifully. I am not certain whether this is simply the result of better concentration or whether there may be some overflow effect in the brain from the areas of concentration to the areas of fine-motor control. There are, of course, other reasons for having poor fine-motor control that will not be changed by the treatment of ADHD.

I have also seen some children who will stop bed-wetting on the very first day of treatment for ADHD. If medication is stopped or missed, the bed-wetting will sometimes recur immediately.

Socially, the milder behaviour problems will improve in days to weeks as self-esteem rises. A common comment by parents is that their child has become much happier as relationships with other children and family members improve. Other people will often comment that a child 'is nicer' on treatment. I emphasize that one is nicer only because one can think better, not because of any effect on mood, activity level, etc. Parents will sometimes tell me that 'we have our child back'.

The questionnaire that follows was completed by the parents of a boy who started treatment at 16 years of age. It demonstrates well the marvelous results that can be seen when treatment is added to the combination of a child who wants to do better and a supportive family. Unfortunately, treatment does not guarantee such wonderful results but the medication does make it more possible.

The second questionnaire also gives a very good indication of what may be seen when the benefits of treatment are put to use. These examples should give a sense of hope to people with children in trouble from ADHD—a demonstration of how much success is possible.

PATIENT #1: √ July 9, 2003 at diagnosis   x July 20, 2004 one year on treatment

ITEMS	Not at all	Just a Little	Pretty Much	Very Much
19. Loses temper.		x		√
20. Argues with adults.	x			√
21. Actively defies or refuses to comply with adult's requests or rules.		x		√
22. Deliberately annoys people.		x		√
23. Blames others for his or her mistakes or misbehaviour	x			√
24. Touchy or easily annoyed by others.	x			√
25. Angry and resentful.	x			√
26. Spiteful or vindictive.	x			√

ATTENTION DEFICIT / HYPERACTIVITY DISORDER

PATIENT #2: √ May 25, 2004 at diagnosis   x July 21, 2004 2 months on treatment

ITEMS	Not at all	Just a Little	Pretty Much	Very Much
1. Fails to give close attention to details or makes careless mistakes in schoolwork, work, or other activities.		x		√
2. Difficulty in sustaining attention in tasks or play activities.		x		√
3. Does not seem to listen when spoken to directly.	x		√	
4. Does not follow through on instructions and fails to finish schoolwork, chores or duties in the workplace (not due to oppositional behaviour or failure to understand instructions)	x			√
5. Difficulty organizing talks and activities.		x		√
6. Avoids, dislikes, or is reluctant to engage in tasks that require sustained mental effort (such as schoolwork or homework).		x		√
7. Loses things necessary for tasks or activities (e.g. toys, school assignments, pencils, books, or tools).	x		√	
8. Easily distracted by extraneous stimuli.		x		√
9. Forgetful in daily activities.		x	√	
10. Fidgets with hands or feet or squirms in seat.		x	√	
11. Leaves seat in classroom or in other situations in which remaining seated is expected.	x	√		
12. Runs about or climbs excessively in situations in which it is inappropriate (in adolescents or adults, may be limited to subjective feelings of restlessness).	x	√		
13. Difficulty playing or engaging in leisure activities quietly.	x		√	

ATTENTION DEFICIT / HYPERACTIVITY DISORDER

PATIENT #2:   √ May 25, 2004 at diagnosis   x July 21, 2004 2 months on treatment

ITEMS	Not at all	Just a Little	Pretty Much	Very Much
14. Is 'on the go" or often acts as if 'driven by a motor'.		x	√	
15. Talks excessively.	√	x		
16. Blurts out answers before questions have been completed.		x √		
17. Has difficulty awaiting turn.		x	√	
18. Interrupts or intrudes on others (e.g., butts into conversations or games)	x			√
19. Loses temper.		x	√	
20. Argues with adults.	x			√
21. Actively defies or refuses to comply with adult's requests or rules.		x		√
22. Deliberately annoys people.		x	√	
23. Blames others for his or her mistakes or misbehaviour.			x	√
24. Touchy or easily annoyed by others.		x	√	
25. Angry and resentful.	x		√	
26. Spiteful or vindictive.	x			√
27. Initiates physical fights	x	√		
28. Has used a weapon that can cause serious physical harm to others (e.g., a bat, brick, broken bottle, knife, gun).	x	√		
29. Has been physically cruel to people.	x	√		
30. Has been physically cruel to animals.	x √			
31. Has stolen while confronting a victim (e.g., mugging, purse snatching, extortion, armed robbery).	x √			
32. Has deliberately engaged in fire setting with the intention of causing serious damage.	x √			
33. Has deliberately destroyed others' property (other than by fire setting).	x			√
34. Has broken into someone else's house, building, or car.	x			√
35. Lies to obtain goods or favours or to avoid obligations (i.e., 'cons' others).			x	√
36. Has stolen items of nontrivial value without confronting a victim (e.g., shoplifting, but without breaking and entering; forgery)	x			√
37. Stays out at night despite parental prohibitions, beginning before age 13 years.	x √			
38. Has run away from home overnight at least twice while living in parental or parental surrogate home (or once).	x √			

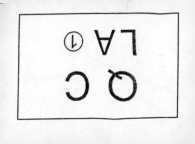

ADHD is a medical condition and, as mentioned, there is a very specific and very effective treatment that can be used to control the problem. Learning disabilities and being a slow learner are diagnosed by psychological evaluation and, unfortunately, there is no specific therapy which is effective. I don't think that one can get as accurate a psychological evaluation of a child with an attentional problem until the attentional problem has been dealt with. Children who cannot focus on the details of psychological testing will not do as well as if they were on therapy. Even though a child with ADHD may be able to sit to do the work with one-to-one help during the testing, the child's thoughts can still wander. Psychologists will sometimes include a comment in the report of an evaluation to point out that 'the result would have been better if the child had been able to focus better'. The psychologist may sometimes find that the results of the many sub-tests carried out are so widely scattered that an accurate evaluation of intelligence cannot be made.

Some children with untreated ADHD, may, on psychological evaluation, be diagnosed with dyslexia. When the ADHD is later diagnosed and treated, the dyslexia may, in some cases, disappear because it wasn't true dyslexia but more likely related to inability to focus on and understand the words. Once treated, children with ADHD often recognize that, prior to treatment, they would have had to read a page four times to be able to understand it. They knew what the words were and they knew what they meant. They didn't have dyslexia. But as their eyes moved down the page, their minds wandered and they couldn't take in what they were reading. **They looked but they could not see.** On treatment, they can read the page once and understand it, simply because they are now able to concentrate and take it in. The same thing happens with things that are said to them - instructions, directions, teaching and requests. **They heard but they couldn't listen.** On treatment they can now take in this information, process it, and act on it.

When I first prescribe medication for ADHD, I give a single test dose. On occasion, parents have called to report that, with that single dose, 'my child sat to read for an hour – and has never done that in his life'.

Some children with ADHD will be identified in school as having **poor reading comprehension.** These children will have difficulty in understanding the meaning of a story they have read and will have difficulty in retelling it and putting events into a logical sequence. The child with ADHD will also tend to have the same difficulty in staying focussed on stories and information they hear as well as those they read – they have **poor listening comprehension.** On treatment, these children can now focus on and take in what they see and hear. Dyslexia can also cause poor reading comprehension but for an entirely different reason – these children have difficulty interpreting and understanding the letters and words. Children with dyslexia will generally have good listening comprehension.

Some children who have been several levels behind their classmates in reading have been able to raise their reading skills by one level a month to catch up to the class reading level – simply because they are now able to take in and understand what they are reading. At the same time, reading becomes more enjoyable because it is so much easier to do.

Because of this improvement in the ability to function and the improved ability to focus on their work, I tell children, when we are discussing treatment, that on the very first day they start therapy for ADHD, they will have less homework because they will now be able to stay focussed in school and to finish classroom work in class. In addition, they will now be able to do any homework better on their own and will no longer need any, or nearly as much, help from parents (this usually brings on a big grin!). This ability to do homework on their own has resulted in more than one child asking teachers for extra homework – being able to do it so much more easily has been so satisfying that these children want even more (most teenagers don't believe me when I tell them this, but I swear that it actually happens).

There are two situations when a child with ADHD will be able to focus better regardless of medication. For any of us, if there is an activity that is of particularly great interest and attraction, we will be able to focus better on it. The same is true for the child with ADHD. If something really interests him, he will be able to focus better at that activity.

The other situation occurs if the child is working one-on-one with somebody who can lead and direct him step by step through an activity. In this situation, distractions have been removed or minimized as well. Teachers will often place a child's desk near theirs to be better able to remind them to stay on task and to avoid distractions. I was recently told about a child with ADHD whose desk was placed beside the teacher's for the entire year in Kindergarten. She found that she had to keep her foot planted firmly on his desk to be able to control and manage him.

As previously mentioned, the diagnosis of ADHD is made on the basis of identification of a sufficient number of characteristics present since before age seven. The severity and number of characteristics tends to diminish as the child gets older. For example, out of a list of fourteen characteristics, one might expect to find ten identified in a child in the early school years. By the time that child is in high school, one may find only six or eight of the fourteen.

Identification of ADHD in a child before school age is essentially impossible because all children have a short attention span until age four or five. There is no method by which we can get the information needed to say that a child meets the requirements to make the diagnosis. However, some preschool children have extreme hyperactivity and significant behaviour problems that need to be addressed.

They can cause severe stress for caregivers and many of these children become very aggressive as a result of constant discipline and lack of acceptance by other children. When other possible causes of hyperactivity have been excluded, I will consider using medication empirically – 'on spec'. Before doing so, however, one has to evaluate the home situation to determine whether parenting techniques, chronic sleep deficit, family stress, etc. may be the cause of behaviour difficulties.

Younger children who are overtired can appear to have ADHD. They will be cranky and irritable, will not be able to think as well and are often hyperactive. Most preschool children require twelve hours of sleep through the night. If they don't get it, their behaviour can mimic ADHD. Sleep deficit is therefore one factor that needs to be addressed in the young child before considering the use of medication.

Active intervention, counselling and parent support will sometimes result in dramatic improvement. When no other cause for the symptoms can be identified, <u>and the child has significant behavioural issues,</u> an empiric trial of medication can be justified. The result of such empiric treatment can be dramatic. (One mother felt that a miracle had happened).

However, I don't think that the diagnosis of ADHD or any other condition can be made by giving a medicine and watching the result – the diagnosis should only be made when accepted criteria are met. Because we cannot meet these criteria in the preschool child, but a dramatic effect has been noted from empiric use of the medicine, I will continue with the treatment until the child enters school and then re-evaluate the diagnosis based on observations in school and at home with the child off treatment for a couple of weeks (or more, if necessary).

Insufficient sleep is one of the things that can mimic ADHD Many younger children who are overtired become overactive. In addition, anyone who is overtired tends to be irritable, fussy, and unable to think as well as one should. There have been studies looking at insufficient rest in adults, using an eight-hour sleep as the desired standard. Intellectual ability is measurably reduced with chronic sleep deficit. One such study showed that in adults, for every hour less than eight on an ongoing basis, IQ dropped 15 points – a very significant effect on function. For example, some adults sleep only six hours a night, night after night. This study suggests that that person's I.Q. is 30 points lower than it should be until a proper sleep pattern is put in place. The effect is quickly reversed with adequate sleep.

It is probably reasonable to assume that this also applies to children and teenagers, who require even longer periods of sleep. I have never met a teenager who likes going to bed or who likes getting up in the morning, and trying to encourage a teenager to get 10 hours sleep is one of a parent's less pleasant tasks

Anxiety is another condition that can closely mimic ADHD. It has been suggested that children brought up in a very chaotic, dysfunctional family in their preschool years may show the signs of ADHD in school. ADHD in one or both parents could possibly contribute either genetically and/or behaviourally to this situation. The symptoms may be related to anxiety arising from their experiences in their early years. In the older child, when ADHD appears to have developed recently, anxiety also needs to be considered as a possible cause.

ADHD will vary from mild to moderate to severe. When one has to decide whether or not medication may be indicated, I don't think the deciding factor is severity. The decision must be based on whether or not the child has a problem from the disorder. If someone with ADHD were living in the middle of the woods and having no problems, there would be no reason to treat. However, even if the disorder is present to only a mild degree but is causing problems, medication needs to be given serious consideration.

Parents will sometimes decide that they would treat on school days only because they want their child to learn. They feel that treatment on non-school days is not necessary because they can manage their child at home. The question that needs to be asked, from the child's point of view, "Is it better to be managed - or better to be able to manage yourself?" It is obvious that being able to manage yourself is what gives you self-esteem, self-confidence and self-assurance. These cannot be taught or given, they have to be earned. This is why there is so much benefit to the child from treatment every day of the year.

CHAPTER VIII
ADHD – TREATMENT OPTIONS

When one is comfortable that the information indicates that the criteria are met and that the child probably has ADHD, and when that ADHD is creating a significant problem for the individual, there are several options to consider:

1. Dietary

For many years it has been argued that something in our diet – some food – causes ADHD. No one has ever identified what that food is. A pediatrician in California back in the 1960s and 1970s felt that he could control ADHD by controlling diet. Nobody has ever been able to duplicate his results using exactly the same diet.

Some people notice that their children become hyperactive when they eat chocolate and have felt that sugar is the cause. There have been many studies in animals and humans evaluating the effect of sugar in the diet. They all point to the fact that sugar, if it does anything at all, calms and quiets - it is not a stimulant. What may be involved for some people, in some artificial chocolate, is red dye. It is also found in brown soft drinks, fruit punch, red popsicles, etc. These children will eat the food, become fairly quickly and very obviously hyperactive for a period of a few hours, and then return to their normal state. ADHD is not primarily hyperactivity; it is an inability to organize thinking. ADHD and this response to red dye have hyperactivity in common, but they are not related. There has never been a food identified that will cause the disorganization of ADHD.

2. Alternative Medicine

Some people feel that if you are going to treat ADHD you should use natural and herbal medicines – that because they are natural and herbal they are automatically going to be safer. The medications included in the natural and herbal group of drugs do not have to go through the same kind of testing and evaluation that prescription drugs do. When you read the claims of the natural and herbal medicines, what they will say is 'People tell us they will do this', 'They are reported to do this'; 'They may do this'. They are not able to say, as one can for a prescription drug, 'This is the active ingredient, this is what it does, these are the side effects, this is the dose'. Someday, there may be a medication found in the natural and herbal group of drugs that will be effective, but so far there has been nothing that has been shown to be consistent and reliable.

3. Stimulant Medications

The two medications that are the mainstay of treatment of ADHD in children have been used for fifty years or more. In fifty years and millions of doses, there are no recognized harmful long-term effects when they are used for ADHD.

I think one of the main reasons that these medications have a bad reputation is that people often don't understand that the medications have a different effect on the person with ADHD than on the person without. The person with ADHD has a biochemical dysfunction that is corrected by the medications and that person is now able to focus and organize his thoughts. The person without

ADHD, who does not have that biochemical problem, becomes stimulated, becomes high, (that is why the medicines are classed as 'stimulant drugs'). The medications are abused for this reason by people who don't have ADHD. The person with ADHD never becomes high. Much of the bad reputation associated with these medicines comes from this abuse by people who don't have ADHD.

We know from fifty years of use that even if you abuse these drugs, you do not become addicted –i.e. they are not addictive drugs.

If you take any medication to make you feel better, you may become psychologically dependent or habituated – stimulant, tranquilizer, antidepressant, marijuana, sedatives, etc. People who take stimulant medications for ADHD feel nothing. The adult is better able to recognize the difference in the way he can think after taking the medication. After taking even the first dose, some adults have described the effect as: 'A cloud has been lifted from my head and for the first time in my life, my thinking has become absolutely clear', but they don't feel anything – there is no pleasurable sensation. Younger children who take it comment that they 'don't have as much homework anymore', that they're 'not in trouble anymore', or that they 'have lots of friends now', but they don't feel anything. Therefore when you take these medications for ADHD they are not even habit forming.

At the moment, there are two medications we can use. They have different chemical structures but the same general effect and same general side effects. Some people do better with one than with the other. At the time of writing, there is a brand new medication that you may have heard about. It has been available in the U.S.A. since January, 2003 but has not as yet been released in Canada. It is not in the stimulant group of drugs and has the potential to be a very valuable addition to our treatment options.

It is reported that its effect lasts for 24 hours. The brand name of this new product is Strattera®.

One of the two currently available drugs is Methylphenidate; commonly know by the trade name of Ritalin®. The other is Dextroamphetamine or Dexedrine® (or Speed on the street for the person who doesn't have ADHD – a completely different effect). The short-acting forms of the medications start to work within twenty or thirty minutes of taking them, act for about four hours, and are out of your body completely in six to eight hours. There is no accumulation or build up from one day to the next and every morning when you get up, you are starting from zero. Because they work for only four hours, you need a dose at breakfast to carry you through the morning, a dose at lunch to carry you through the afternoon, and many people benefit from a dose late in the afternoon

Both medications have preparations that will last eight hours (Ritalin SR® and Dexedrine Spansules®) which make it possible to avoid the need for a dose at lunch time, a feature that is popular for teenagers who hate having peers know that they take medication. When taking these forms, a dose of short-acting medication is often taken later in the afternoon.

Two new formulations have been developed to extend the effect of medication even further – Concerta® (Methylphenidate) and AdderallXR® (Dextro – and Levoamphetamine) which are active for 12 hours or more. Many people find that the effect is smoother and appreciate the benefit of having it last through until early evening, especially welcomed by teenagers.

The main side effect of the medicines is that they cut down on appetite. To reduce this, we give the short- acting forms with meals. When one gets up in the morning, there is no effect left from the day before, so the child has a normal appetite at breakfast. The first dose is taken with breakfast, starts to work 20-30 minutes later and the meal has been finished. The breakfast dose will cut down on the appetite at lunchtime and it has to be accepted that children will not eat as much at that meal. (This effect tends to diminish as one reaches adulthood.) However the noon hour dose has worn off enough that by suppertime, appetite should be back and the child will be able to eat well again. Those children who do not feel like eating at lunchtime will often drink. Giving them whole milk at lunch will provide much more and better nutrition than juice or soft drink and will help to offset the effect of the appetite suppression.

We need to monitor weight to make sure that children continue to eat enough to gain weight normally. It used to be thought that children who took the medicine year round would not grow as tall as they otherwise might. It is now realized that this is related primarily to nutrition, and as long as they eat enough to gain normally they should grow normally. This is generally not a big problem, but it does need to be followed. As with any prescription drug, there is ongoing monitoring and evaluation to ensure that no unrecognized effects are identified.

When the medicine is first started, some people will complain of cramps, stomach ache, nausea, - a mild stomach upset that usually disappears in the first week. If the symptoms should continue beyond the first week, another medication should be tried.

Some children will get tics, muscle twitching or nervous habits such as nail biting as a side-effect of the medicine. This, fortunately, seldom happens, but if it does, it needs to be recognized so that something can be done about it. The tics, if they are related to the medication, will stop when the medication is stopped. Stimulant drugs may accentuate or precipitate the tics of Tourette's syndrome but there is no evidence that they will cause them. Stress itself is a more common cause of tics than the medications used to treat ADHD.

The medication can make some children very sensitive and very emotional. They are often emotional before starting treatment because life has just generally not been that successful for them. As they start to do better on treatment the emotionality should go. If it doesn't, we have to consider whether the medication may be contributing to it.

One of the bad things that is said about the medication is that people who take it are spaced out and 'zombied'. This is true only if the dose is too high. We are not treating children to make them calm and quiet; we are treating them to focus. If they seem "lost in space" on treatment, we need to evaluate the dose of medication they are receiving, as it may be too high.

Parents will sometimes comment that their child is quiet after the medication has been taken. The quietness probably comes from the fact they now have only a single thought in their head instead of many, and are able to sit and focus on one idea at a time. They will be still be able to respond quickly and appropriately to requests, etc.

As mentioned, many people benefit from a dose of medication late afternoon. If there is an activity at which they have to focus (homework, studying, swimming class, Guides or Scouts or a team sport), these children will be able to focus better. Many children who are on hockey, soccer or other teams tell me that they are much better players if they've had their medication prior to the game. They are not physically better, but can be better team players because they can stay focussed on the game. The importance of this is not to make children into superstars, but if you are a member of a team and have the respect of teammates, it does wonders for one's own self-esteem. This is the most important reason for identifying and treating ADHD.

Some people seem to have increased difficulty in falling asleep on treatment and this can interfere with its use. ADHD itself can make it difficult for children to fall asleep because their minds are racing and it is not easy to settle down. Many children with

ADHD will actually go to sleep better with a dose late in the afternoon, not because they are calmed or quieted, but because their minds are no longer as active.

The new formulations that act for 12 hours provide control of ADHD through the day, after school and into the early evening with only one dose at breakfast. It much easier for everyone to have to remember only one dose a day. It also improves the parents' ability to supervise and maintain control of the medication.

We must remember that current medications have no effect remaining on waking in the morning and every morning the characteristics and behaviours of ADHD will be present. This means that most children will have great difficulty in remembering to take their medication and therefore reminders and supervision by a parent is often necessary to ensure that the pill is taken. The new drug, Strattera®, may provide additional help with this.

The dosage range of the medication is quite wide. My approach to starting the medication is to give a test dose just below the middle of the dosage range, based on weight, recognizing that the dose may need to be adjusted slightly to get the full benefit. If further experience shows that the dose used does not allow the child to focus well, or does not last the appropriate length of time, it may need to be increased. This will need fine-tuning based on the response of each individual, for we all vary to some degree in our response to medication. As a child grows and gains weight, the dose will need to be gradually increased. This will become apparent when the child begins to have the original symptoms return - unfinished classroom work, inappropriate behaviour, restlessness, etc.

Some people metabolize drugs more slowly than the average person. This may result in a stronger action for these individuals and they will require a lower-than-average dose for the desired effect. There are also children who are rapid metabolizers and who will need higher-than-average or more frequent doses.

The results of even the first dose of medication are useful in assuring that treatment will be beneficial and I ask parents to give that first dose themselves and to watch their child for the next three to four hours. This is to ensure that nothing happens that we don't want – especially that the child is not stimulated. Many parents comment on how pleasant their child became, that there was a rapid improvement in how the child related to other children, or that they were able to sit down and have a very enjoyable conversation, even with that first single dose.

4. Behaviour Management

Over the years, there have been many studies to compare the treatment of children with ADHD using stimulant medication alone, behavior management alone, or both forms of treatment in combination. The results have consistently shown that if one were to use a single treatment approach only, the use of medication alone far exceeds the results from behaviour management alone. Behaviour management techniques, counselling and discipline cannot be used effectively until a child is able to think before acting. Otherwise the child will not be able to use the strategies learned. This goes back to the question – 'Is it better to be managed or to be able to manage yourself?'

For many children, particularly if diagnosed and treated in the early years of school, this improved ability to think better and to succeed socially and academically may be the only treatment necessary. For those children who have other factors contributing to their problem, the low self-esteem and these other factors can result in behaviour and conduct disorders that may well require behavior management and counseling along with medical treatment.

Behaviour management programs and counselling cannot be as successful unless the child is a willing participant and able to remember, think and use the skills being taught. Without medication to be able organize the child's thinking process, there will be no meaningful improvement from behaviour management strategies and the child will tend to stop trying. When counselling is indicated, it will be much more successful when combined with medication.

Treatment of children with ADHD does not make them into perfect children and it goes without saying that these children require the same parenting as any child – rules, standards, example, expectations, discipline, etc.

When a diagnosis of ADHD has been made on the basis of good information and when one is comfortable that the criteria have been met, the remarkable response to treatment is simply further support that the diagnosis is accurate. However, response to treatment should never be the basis for the diagnosis.

Most children who start on medication for ADHD will continue with it through the school years. The decision whether or not to continue beyond that time is best made by the patients themselves because, as young adults, they can so much better recognize the difference in the way they can think. They can thereby make a better judgment as to whether the benefits to them outweigh the nuisance and negative aspects of taking any medication. The commonest comment that parents make to me after they have seen their child on treatment is 'I've got my child back'. One boy told me that, without his pill, his head 'is full of little green snakes but that they go to somebody else' after he takes his medicine. I have been told that some children at five or six years of age, when their medication has been forgotten, will ask their parent for the pill 'because it makes it easier for me to think.'

CHAPTER IX
ADHD – ADDITIONAL COMMENTS

Several studies have been done to evaluate teenagers with ADHD and driving. They consistently show that they are much safer drivers and much less likely to have an accident if they have taken their medication. On treatment, as one would expect, they will be able to concentrate better, be less likely to be distracted and less impulsive. It has been recently recognized that this observation also applies to adults with ADHD.

It has been said over the years that we should not use these abused drugs in young children as they will be more likely to abuse drugs in later years because they will have no respect for them. This claim has been studied in recent years and it would appear that there is no basis for it. What was found was that people treated from the time they are young are <u>less likely</u> to abuse substances, including alcohol, because they feel so good about themselves.

ADHD is an extremely satisfying condition to treat. As mentioned, the only thing we do with treatment is to **let** the child think better - we don't **make** the child do anything – we don't **help** the child do anything – the successes that the child experiences are the child's successes. When marks on report cards rise significantly and when the child now has more friends, the smile on the face and self-confidence shown by the child is strong evidence that life has become much better.

After going over this information in the office with the parents of a child with ADHD, very often one parent (and sometimes both) will say; 'you are talking about me!'- Only then do some people begin to recognize the reasons for the difficulties they have had all their lives – inability to hold down a job – dropping out of school – low self-esteem – inappropriate behaviours and marital problems. Many of these adults have been diagnosed with dyslexia, anxiety, depression or other disorders. There is increasing recognition by psychiatrists that ADHD is not uncommon as a cause of adult behaviour problems and more and more adults are having medication recommended for them.

Difficulty in paying attention can be found as a characteristic of other disorders as well. Bipolar Disorder (one type of depression), Fetal Alcohol Syndrome, Tourette's Syndrome and Fragile X Syndrome are some examples of these other disorders. Inattentiveness is not the most significant part of these other conditions and there are other specific features to indicate that this is something other than ADHD.

The children I see in the office are referred because someone has recognized that characteristics of ADHD may be the cause of their problems. These problems often include social difficulties. On treatment for ADHD and the improved ability to recognize consequences and organize thinking, these social problems often improve dramatically and quickly. However, some children continue to have significant social problems even after the ADHD has been controlled. If you know a child who has been treated for ADHD but who continues to have difficulty in making and keeping friends, the following information may be helpful.

When one looks into the history of such a child, there are often indications of difficulty in playing with other children even at two, three or four years of age. These children are often described as 'loners' – they would 'parallel play' rather than interact at play with other children, even in daycare. These children may have a second disorder co-existing with ADHD. As babies, they are sometimes recognized by parents as being 'different'. They may not have liked to be cuddled – they may not have played 'peek-a-boo' or 'pat-a-cake'.

As older children, they may develop an overwhelming interest in specific topics and will spend hours playing, talking about or reading books or watching TV. – cars, trucks, fire engines, astronomy, maps, dinosaurs, Egypt….the list can be endless. The child often becomes extremely knowledgeable about a particular subject and can recite statistics and details. The topic may change from week to week or from one month to the next.

These children sometimes develop very fixed routines that they have to follow – the steps taken to go to bed or to get up in the morning, positioning toys, belongings or animals on the bed – not accepting food on the plate if one food touches another – the route they follow on the way to or from school. They may have unusual motor activities or repeat words or actions to the point of annoyance. They may read out loud in a monotone.

When these additional characteristics are present, one has to ask whether ADHD explains only part of the child's problem and whether a disorder called Autism Spectrum Disorder needs to be considered as well.

Autism has been recognized for many years as a very, very severe condition where children live in their own world and show little interest in anyone else. We have long recognized children who had some of the features of Autism but were not severe enough to consider this as a diagnosis. It is now realized that Autism varies from this very severe form to much milder forms and is much more common than had been realized in the past. Because of the wide variation in severity and differences in how it may appear, the group of conditions is now called Autism Spectrum Disorder (A.S.D.) and can be subdivided into:

- Autistic Disorder (AUT. DIS).
- Asperger's Disorder (ASP. DIS.)
- Pervasive Developmental Disorder – Not Otherwise Specified (PDD- NOS)
- Childhood Disintegrative Disorder, etc.

Children with Autistic Disorder have difficulties in three areas:
1. Social interaction
2. Communication
3. Restricted, repetitive and stereotypic behaviour and interests

The difficulties with language are evident in learning to talk and children with AUT. DIS. do not even begin to say meaningful words until age two or to use phrases until age three.

Asperger's Disorder is a condition related to AUT. DIS. which results in the same social problems. Children with ASP. DIS. have difficulties in the social area and in the behaviour and interests area, but not with language. Children with ASP. DIS may have superior intelligence, sometimes with almost unbelievable knowledge in specific areas.

Children with ASP. DIS. or AUT. DIS. are at increased risk of also having ADHD and may be first seen by a physician for the ADHD. As with ADHD, there is unfortunately no specific test that can diagnose ASP. DIS. or AUT. DIS. – diagnosis is based on recognition of enough of the characteristics to meet established criteria. (See tables 3 and 4)

At this time, there is no medication that is useful in treating ASP. DIS. or AUT. DIS. as there is for ADHD. Much research is being carried out by pharmaceutical companies to try to find an effective medication and there is reason to think and hope that one may be found in the future. However it is very important to recognize these disorders as these children can be helped to be more successful in life by developing programs to help them academically and to teach them social skills. With help, these children can learn how to respond and be better accepted in their relationships with others. This help can be provided in the home, at school and at camps where social skills are taught.

Children with the more severe forms of Autistic Disorder have been shown to benefit from very intensive teaching, patterning and training programs and close support, especially when begun in the early stages of development. Children with the milder forms are often not recognized until the early school years or even later and do not require as intensive a program as the more severe forms.

Recognition that this disorder is present gives caregivers a better understanding of how to manage the child. For example, the child with ASP. DIS. or AUT. DIS. will strongly resist being pushed or forced or told to do something but will usually respond much better to being led. Instead of forcefully telling the child to clean up a mess he left in the living room, one will get a better response by asking him to pick things up 'to help make the room look tidier'.

When a child with ADHD is appropriately treated and continues to have these kinds of difficulties in interpersonal relationships, the possibility of mild. ASP. DIS. or AUT. DIS. must be considered. The child with mild to moderate degrees of these disorders will benefit enormously from programs to address any academic or social problems along with treatment for ADHD. People with a less severe presentation of ASP. DIS or AUT. DIS. who are provided with support can do very well in life. Graduation from high school and university is within their reach and job security, marriage and family are all possible with support along with treatment of ADHD when they co-exist.

Table 3: DSM - IV Criteria for Autistic Disorder

A - Total of at least six items from (1), (2), and (3), with at least two from (1), and one each from (2) and (3):

1. Qualitive impairment in social interaction, as manifested by at least two of the following:

1) Marked impairment in the use of multiple nonverbal behaviours, such as eye-to-eye gaze, facial expression, body postures, and gestures to regulate social interaction.

2) Failure to develop peer relationships appropriate to developmental level.

3) A lack of spontaneous seeking to share enjoyment, interests, or achievements with other people (e.g., by a lack of showing, bringing, or pointing out objects of interest).

4) Lack of social or emotional reciprocity.

2. Qualitive impairments in communication, as manifested by at least one of the following:

a) Delay in, or total lack of, the development of spoken language (not accompanied by an attempt to compensate through alternative modes of communication such as gestures or mime).

b) In individuals with adequate speech, marked impairment in the ability to initiate or sustain a conversation with others.

c) Stereotyped and repetitive use of language or idiosyncratic language.

d) Lack of varied spontaneous make-believe play or social imitative play appropriate to developmental level.

3. Restricted, repetitive, and stereotyped patterns of behaviour, interests, and activities, as manifested by at least one of the following:

a) Encompassing preoccupation with one or more stereotyped and restricted patterns of interest that is abnormal either in intensity of focus.

b) Apparently inflexible adherence to specific, nonfunctional routines or rituals.

c) Stereotyped and repetitive motor mannerisms (e.g., hand or finger flapping or twisting or complex whole body movements.

d) Persistent preoccupation with parts of objects.

B. - Delays or abnormal functioning in at least one of the following areas, with onset prior to age 3 years:

1. Social interaction

2. Language as used in social communication

3. Symbolic or imaginative play

C. - Not better accounted for by Rett disorder or childhood disintegrative disorder.

Table 4: DSM - IV Criteria for Asperger Disorder

A - Qualitive impairment in social interaction, as manifested by at least two of the following:
1) Marked impairment in the use of multiple nonverbal behaviours, such as eye-to-eye gaze, facial expression, body postures, and gestures to regulate social interaction.
2) Failure to develop peer relationships appropriate to developmental level.
3) A lack of spontaneous seeking to share enjoyment, interests, or achievements with other people (e.g., by a lack of showing, bringing, or pointing out objects of interest).
4) Lack of social or emotional reciprocity.
B - Restricted, repetitive, and stereotyped patterns of behaviour, interests, and activities, as manifested by at least one of the following:
1) Encompassing preoccupation with one or more stereotyped and restricted patterns of interest that is abnormal either in intensity or focus.
2) Apparently inflexible adherence to specific, nonfunctional routines or rituals.
3) Stereotyped and repetitive motor mannerisms (e.g. hand or finger flapping or twisting or complex whole-body movements.
4) Persistent preoccupation with parts of objects.
C.- The disturbance causes clinically significant impairment in social, occupational, or other important areas of functioning.
D.- There is no clinically significant general delay in language (e.g. single words used by age 2 years, communicative phrases used by age 3 years).
E.- There is no clinically significant delay in cognitive development or in the development of age-appropriate self-help skills, adaptive hehaviour (other than in social interaction), and curiosity about the environment in childhood.
F.- Criteria are not met for another pervasive developmental disorder or schizophrenia.

In the Fall of 2003, our son was assessed and diagnosed with ADHD. We placed him on medication for the ADHD after some soul-searching. Although many people have differing views on this issue (as we have found through personal experience) for him the medication has changed his life. He is now able to concentrate on one task for hours instead of seconds.

However he continued to have problems in getting along with the other children. It was finally recognized that he has Asperger's Disorder as well as ADHD. My wife and I were dumbfounded and distraught that our little boy had such a major problem. Our son was always extremely hyperactive, had major aggression issues and very poor social skills. Although we knew there was a problem with him, we were worried that if our friends and family found out that our boy was diagnosed with an Autism Spectrum Disorder, he would be labeled by them and left permanently scarred with insecurity. We worried that he would not be able to function at school and might not be as well educated as his mother and I would like him to be. We thought about his long term future and were caught thinking that his life would be an uphill struggle.

Our thoughts have changed since that time last Fall. We have worked with a social worker and behaviour specialist and learned how to change our environment for the betterment of our son. Our son struggles with transitioning from one task to another, so we let him know when a transition is coming. If that leads to a temper tantrum, we have learned how to redirect to another task. My wife and I have found that he still struggles in environments were there are many people or children – thus we try to limit the number of kids he plays with to one at a time and we try to limit the size of the group activity so that it is easier for him to function.

He has been able to function very well in kindergarten and we are proud to say that his social and behavioural issues are getting better every single day.

For parents who are discouraged – we have walked in your shoes. We can proudly boast that, by learning to think as our child with Asperger's thinks, our life has improved markedly.

Parents of a four year old

FINAL WORDS

For many years, ADHD was treated on school days only with good academic effect. Unfortunately, failure to recognize the social impact of ADHD resulted in so many of these children continuing to have marked behavioural difficulties and very poor outcomes as teenagers and adults.

Now that we have this understanding, we can offer children with ADHD and their families a course of therapy that allows them to learn and develop without a cloud of disorganization and foggy thinking interfering with their success. A child with ADHD can have severe stress in trying to manage in life and can create severe stress for a family. Diagnosis and treatment before age 8-10 will increase the success rate.

It is my hope that this information will help you to understand what ADHD is – and what it isn't - and to be more comfortable with the idea of medication, its good and bad points and its powerful role in letting children with ADHD become more successful.

There will be times in many families when a child or a parent will raise the question of whether treatment could be stopped. Teenagers in particular may begin to resist – they want to 'be themselves'. Younger children may suddenly show no effect from treatment because they are not swallowing the medicine (some children will tuck the pill in the pocket of the cheek, behind the back teeth, and then go to the bathroom and spit it out). When the question of whether or not to continue treatment has been raised, it may help to stop treatment for a short time to allow re-assessment of the child's ability to function on his own. It usually becomes quickly obvious that the benefits of treatment far outweigh the nuisance of having to take medication and its side-effects. Whenever one is deciding about taking any medication, the good effects of the medicine must be measured against the bad – all medications have both.

We know that these medications can:

1. Decrease appetite – primarily only at lunch time and quite easily managed, but weight and height need to be monitored.

2. May interfere with falling asleep. ADHD itself often makes it difficult to settle to sleep. People with untreated ADHD will often say that their thoughts are racing when they try to sleep and they often don't get to sleep easily. Adequate rest is important and medication to gently allow the child to settle will provide the benefit of treatment as well as adequate rest.

3. Some children may have unusual sensations on first starting medication. These usually last for only a few days and then disappear. Should such unusual feelings persist, an adjustment of the dose or another medication should be tried before assuming that treatment should not be continued.

4. When a child has had to cope with ADHD for several years before the condition is recognized, it is sometimes difficult for that child to know and accept who he really is – the person who cannot organize his thoughts without medication or the organized individual on medication. Some of these children, especially teenagers, will feel that they don't need their medication – that they can do equally well on their own. Fortunately, they

usually quickly recognize if they stop treatment that in fact, they are able to function much better on treatment and will more willingly continue.

Very often, parents, teachers and others in contact with a child with ADHD are aware of how much better the child can do on therapy. The child himself needs to be aware of this. We cannot force anyone to take medication – the patient has to be willing. When dealing with a child who resists treatment, patience, understanding and repetition of the information will usually result in agreement to continue to take the prescription. It is extremely disappointing and sad when someone absolutely refuses, in spite of all efforts, as we know that the child is making a decision that can put at risk a successful outcome, both academically and socially.

Because the dose of any medication will vary depending on body size, the dose of medication will need to be increased as the child gains weight and grows.

TREATMENT BY ITSELF IS NO GUARANTEE OF SUCCESS but it allows the child with ADHD to make better use of his or her abilities and thereby certainly improves the opportunity for a happy and successful adult outcome.

Goodbye Dr. Burgh
Thank you for everything.
I'll miss you !!

Keith

When I was asked to write the story of my diagnosis with ADHD, I quickly agreed in hopes that this story, if not this book, will help people better understand the disorder. I grew up hearing the term 'ADHD' without ever really knowing what it was. I, like most people around me at the time, believed that someone with ADHD was an extremely hyperactive person who could not sit still for more than 30 seconds at a time, and was basically not normal.

Growing up, I always had trouble in school. I'm not saying I failed any classes, but I couldn't sit and listen to my teacher and concentrate on what they were saying for more than ten minutes before I would begin to daydream. Many of my teachers caught this, but only assumed that I didn't care about school and I was a daydreamer, and because I was "normal" no one ever thought I could possibly have ADHD.

When I began to learn more about ADHD and its signs and symptoms, I started thinking that I might have it. When I tried to discuss this with other people, they would not believe me and told me that it's impossible for me to have ADHD; I wasn't disruptive enough to have the disorder. People simply believed that I didn't study and/or try hard enough and that's why my marks in school were low.

I remember not being able to read two pages of a book without having to go back and reread them because I wasn't able to follow the story. Again people would just tell me that I didn't try hard enough and wasn't reading interesting books. No one seemed to believe and/or accept that I might have ADHD.

Finally after two years of trying to get people to listen to my suspicion that I might have ADHD, I was evaluated for it. According to all evidence, the doctor told me it was a definite possibility that I could have this disorder but that the main test for me would be to see how I would react when taking the medication. I must say that taking the medication was one of the toughest things I ever had to do in my life. If I took the pill and it had no effect on me, I would have to face the fact that I was what everyone had labeled me: 'a non-motivated lazy daydreamer'. However, if the medication did have an effect on me, it would open many doors for me that were never open before.

After taking the pill I didn't notice any difference. However, I tried reading and was able to do it without any difficulty, and people around me said they noticed a difference in my attitude almost instantly. They said I was more agreeable and easier to get along with.

My marks in school started to go up and I found it easier to concentrate in school and take notes. My interest in school was heightened and I found myself able to concentrate better and studying was no longer a seemingly impossible task. It felt like my potential was finally being unlocked and I was able to work to the best of my abilities.

At the time of the diagnosis and first starting the medicine, I was in my fifth year of working on my B.A, and 22 years old. I am now in a Masters Program, making top marks and enjoying it.

I am not ashamed of my disorder nor do I blame it for any of my downfalls – I accept it and have no problem living with it. I have always had this attitude toward my disorder, even when I was first diagnosed. At first, due to this, I was not afraid to tell people that I have ADHD and told my family that they could tell anyone also. However, after about two months of being diagnosed, I asked my family to no longer tell people I have ADHD, I also became careful to whom I revealed the diagnosis.

As I said before, it is not that I am ashamed of this disorder; it is other people's reaction to it that made me stop and think. After I would tell people, they would look at me differently and treated me as if I was beneath them. I began to realize that a certain stigma comes with being diagnosed with ADHD. Unfortunately, people still view it as a disorder that affects only those 'out of control' kids and people with extreme personality disorders.

My hopes in writing this is that people will realize that this disorder is real and that it can affect people in different ways. Treatment is truly beneficial and worthwhile. No one would even know I have

ADHD unless I tell them, so how come when I tell people I have ADHD I am automatically ostracized and seen as different? Unfortunately, until other people stop associating ADHD with wild behaviours and personality problems, those diagnosed with it (myself included) will have to hide our disorder. It is for this reason that I have written this anonymously, I am not embarrassed about it, I am more afraid of other peoples' reaction.

A university student

If the information in this book or that from other sources suggests that your child, or children, may be having difficulties as a result of ADHD, I would suggest that a good next step would be to look at the report cards from kindergarten to grade VI to see if there are consistent comments about:
- Difficulty concentrating and focussing
- Needing much teacher support or 1:1 to stay on task
- Distracted
- Not able to stay seated or disrupts others by fidgeting or talking
- Blurts out in class
- Doesn't recognize the consequences of his action

If such comments have been made from year to year (perhaps less likely in kindergarten), a further evaluation by your physician would be valuable.

ABOUT THE AUTHOR

Dr. Rod Bergh graduated in medicine from Dalhousie University, Halifax, NS and spent three years in Oromocto, NB before starting a paediatric residency at the University of Michigan Medical Centre, Ann Arbor, MI.

He was then in private practice in Fredericton, NB providing both primary care and consultation services in paediatrics.

From 1980 to 1985, he was a consultant paediatrician at Tawam Hospital in the United Arab Emirates.

On his return to Canada, he went to Sudbury, ON as Coordinator of Paediatric Services at Laurentian Hospital and to practice as a consultant paediatrician. He was Chief of Medical Staff at Laurentian Hospital from 1986 to 1998.

During his time in Sudbury, he was involved with the development of the Northern Ontario Family Medicine Program.

In 1999, Dr. Bergh relocated to Ottawa, ON in a practice devoted to children with learning difficulties. As their children are no longer at home, his wife works with him to determine whether or not characteristics of ADHD are contributing to the learning problem.

Dr. Bergh has been closely involved with The Canadian Paediatric Society and was President of the Society in 1973-74. He has been Chairman of the Paediatric Practice Committee, The Education Committee and MOCOMP and CME Committees, Editor of The CPS New Bulletin from 1985 to 1990 and liaison member to The American Academy of Pediatric Education Committee and PREP Advisory Committee and representative to The Royal College MOCOMP Committee.

Dr. Bergh's experience with ADHD has been developed over several years of direct clinical contact in diagnosing, treating and following children with the disorder.

INDEX
EXPLAINING ADHD

Printed and bounded in September 2004 at Gauvin Press
Gatineau, Quebec